THE BALLAD OF THE WHITE HORSE

G. K. CHESTERTON

D1432792

DOVER PUBLICATIONS, INC.
MINEOLA, NEW YORK

TO

MY WIFE

Bibliographical Note

This Dover edition, first published in 2010, is an unabridged republication of the work originally published by John Lane Company, New York, in 1911.

Library of Congress Cataloging-in-Publication Data

Chesterton, G. K. (Gilbert Keith), 1874-1936.
    The ballad of the white horse / G.K. Chesterton. —Dover ed.
      p. cm.
    ISBN-13: 978-0-486-47563-9 (pbk.)
    ISBN-10: 0-486-47563-8 (pbk.)
    1. Alfred, King of England, 849-899—Poetry. 2. Great Britain—History—Alfred, 871-899—Poetry. 3. White Horse, Vale of (England) —Poetry. 4. Christian poetry. I. Title.

PR4453.C4B2 2010
821'.912—dc22

                        2010005024

Manufactured in the United States by LSC Communications
47563807   2019
www.doverpublications.com

PREFATORY NOTE

THIS ballad needs no historical notes, for the simple reason that it does not profess to be historical. All of it that is not frankly fictitious, as in any prose romance about the past, is meant to emphasize tradition rather than history. King Alfred is not a legend in the sense that King Arthur may be a legend; that is, in the sense that he may possibly be a lie. But King Alfred is a legend in this broader and more human sense, that the legends are the most important things about him.

The cult of Alfred was a popular cult, from the darkness of the ninth century to the deepening twilight of the twentieth. It is wholly as a popular legend that I deal with him here. I write as one ignorant of everything, except that I have found the legend of a King of Wessex still alive in the land. I will give three curt cases of what I mean. A tradition connects the ultimate victory of Alfred with the valley in Berkshire called the Vale of the White Horse. I have seen doubts of the tradition, which may be valid doubts. I do not know when or where the story started; it is enough that it started somewhere and ended with me; for I only seek to write upon a hearsay, as the old balladists did. For the second case, there is a popular tale that Alfred played the harp and sang in the Danish camp; I select it because it is a popular tale, at whatever time it arose. For the third case, there is a popular tale that Alfred came in contact with a woman and cakes; I select it because it is a popular tale, because it is a vulgar one. It has been disputed by grave historians, who were, I think, a little too grave to be good judges of it. The two chief charges against the story are that it was first recorded long after Alfred's death, and that (as Mr. Oman urges) Alfred never really wandered all alone without any thanes or soldiers. Both these objections might possibly be met. It has taken us nearly as long to learn the whole truth about Byron, and perhaps longer to learn the whole truth about Pepys, than elapsed between Alfred and the first writing of such tales. And as for the other objection, do the historians really think that Alfred after Wilton, or Napoleon after Leipsic, never walked about in a wood by himself for the matter of an hour or two? Ten

PREFATORY NOTE

minutes might be made sufficient for the essence of the story. But I am not concerned to prove the truth of these popular traditions. It is enough for me to maintain two things: that they are popular traditions; and that without these popular traditions we should have bothered about Alfred about as much as we bother about Eadwig.

One other consideration needs a note. Alfred has come down to us in the best way (that is, by national legends) solely for the same reason as Arthur and Roland and the other giants of that darkness, because he fought for the Christian civilization against the heathen nihilism. But since this work was really done by generation after generation, by the Romans before they withdrew, and by the Britons while they remained, I have summarised this first crusade in a triple symbol, and given to a fictitious Roman, Celt, and Saxon, a part in the glory of Ethandune. I fancy that in fact Alfred's Wessex was of very mixed bloods; but in any case, it is the chief value of legend to mix up the centuries while preserving the sentiment; to see all ages in a sort of splendid foreshortening. That is the use of tradition: it telescopes history.

G. K. C.

CONTENTS

DEDICATION

Of great limbs gone to chaos,
  A great face turned to night —
Why bend above a shapeless shroud
Seeking in such archaic cloud
  Sight of strong lords and light?

Where seven sunken Englands
  Lie buried one by one,
Why should one idle spade, I wonder,
Shake up the dust of thanes like thunder
  To smoke and choke the sun?

In cloud of clay so cast to heaven
  What shape shall man discern?
These lords may light the mystery
Of mastery or victory,
And these ride high in history,
  But these shall not return.

DEDICATION

Gored on the Norman gonfalon
  The Golden Dragon died;
We shall not wake with ballad strings
The good time of the smaller things,
We shall not see the holy kings
  Ride down by Severn side.

Stiff, strange, and quaintly coloured
  As the broidery of Bayeux
The England of that dawn remains,
And this of Alfred and the Danes
Seems like the tales a whole tribe feigns,
  Too English to be true.

Of a good king on an island
  That ruled once on a time;
And as he walked by an apple tree
There came green devils out of the sea
With sea-plants trailing heavily
  And tracks of opal slime.

Yet Alfred is no fairy tale;
  His days as our days ran,
He also looked forth for an hour
On peopled plains and skies that lower,
From those few windows in the tower
  That is the head of a man.

DEDICATION

But who shall look from Alfred's hood
　　Or breathe his breath alive?
His century like a small dark cloud
Drifts far; it is an eyeless crowd,
Where the tortured trumpets scream aloud
　　And the dense arrows drive.

Lady, by one light only
　　We look from Alfred's eyes,
We know he saw athwart the wreck
The sign that hangs about your neck,
Where One more than Melchizedek
　　Is dead and never dies.

Therefore I bring these rhymes to you,
　　Who brought the cross to me,
Since on you flaming without flaw
I saw the sign that Guthrum saw
When he let break his ships of awe,
　　And laid peace on the sea.

Do you remember when we went
　　Under a dragon moon,
And 'mid volcanic tints of night
Walked where they fought the unknown fight
And saw black trees on the battle-height,
　　Black thorn on Ethandune?

DEDICATION

And I thought, "I will go with you,
  As man with God has gone,
And wander with a wandering star,
The wandering heart of things that are,
The fiery cross of love and war
  That like yourself, goes on."

O go you onward; where you are
  Shall honour and laughter be,
Past purpled forest and pearled foam,
God's winged pavilion free to roam,
Your face, that is a wandering home,
  A flying home for me.

Ride through the silent earthquake lands,
  Wide as a waste is wide,
Across these days like deserts, when
Pride and a little scratching pen
Have dried and split the hearts of men,
  Heart of the heroes, ride.

Up through an empty house of stars,
  Being what heart you are,
Up the inhuman steeps of space
As on a staircase go in grace,
Carrying the firelight on your face
  Beyond the loneliest star.

DEDICATION

Take these; in memory of the hour
  We strayed a space from home
And saw the smoke-hued hamlets, quaint
With Westland king and Westland saint,
And watched the western glory faint
  Along the road to Frome.

G. K. C.

BOOK I

THE VISION OF THE KING

THE BALLAD OF THE WHITE HORSE

THE VISION OF THE KING

BEFORE the gods that made the gods
　　Had seen their sunrise pass,
The White Horse of the White Horse Vale
　　Was cut out of the grass.

Before the gods that made the gods
　　Had drunk at dawn their fill,
The White Horse of the White Horse Vale
　　Was hoary on the hill.

Age beyond age on British land,
　　Æons on æons gone,
Was peace and war in western hills,
　　And the White Horse looked on.

For the White Horse knew England
　　When there was none to know;
He saw the first oar break or bend,
He saw heaven fall and the world end,
　　O God, how long ago!

For the end of the world was long ago,
  And all we dwell to-day
Like children of some second birth,
Like a strange people left on earth
  After a judgment day.

For the end of the world was long ago,
  When the ends of the world waxed free,
When Rome was sunk in a waste of slaves,
  And the sun drowned in the sea.

When Cæsar's sun fell out of the sky,
  And whoso hearkened right
Could only hear the plunging
  Of the nations in the night.

When the ends of the earth came marching in
  To torch and cresset gleam,
And the roads of the world that lead to Rome
Were filled with faces that moved like foam,
  Like faces in a dream.

And men rode out of the eastern lands,
  Broad river and burning plain;
Trees that are Titan flowers to see,
And tiger skies, striped horribly,
  With tints of tropic rain.

THE VISION OF THE KING

Where Ind's enamelled peaks arise
  Around that inmost one,
Where ancient eagles on its brink,
Vast as archangels, gather and drink
  The sacrament of the sun.

And men brake out of the northern lands,
  Enormous lands alone,
Where a spell is laid upon life and lust
And the rain is changed to a silver dust
  And the sea to a great green stone.

And a Shape that moveth murkily
  In mirrors of ice and night,
Hath blanched with fear all beasts and birds,
As death and a shock of evil words
  Blast a man's hair with white.

And the cry of the palms and the purple moons,
  Or the cry of the frost and foam,
Swept ever around an inmost place,
And the din of distant race on race
  Cried and replied round Rome.

And there was death on the Emperor
  And night upon the Pope;
And Alfred, hiding in deep grass,
  Hardened his heart with hope.

A sea-folk blinder than the sea
   Broke all about his land;
And Alfred up against them bare
And gripped the ground and grasped the air,
   Staggered, and strove to stand.

He bent them back with spear and spade,
   With desperate dyke and wall,
With foemen leaning on his shield
And roaring on him when he reeled;
   And no help came at all.

He broke them with a broken sword
   A little towards the sea;
And for one hour of panting peace,
Ringed with a roar that would not cease,
With golden crown and girded fleece
   Made laws under a tree.

    .   .   .   .

The Northmen came about our land
   A Christless chivalry:
Who knew not of the arch or pen,
Great, beautiful, half-witted men
   From the sunrise and the sea.

Misshapen ships stood on the deep
   Full of strange gold and fire,

6

THE VISION OF THE KING

And hairy men, as huge as sin,
With hornèd heads, came wading in
  Through the long, low sea-mire.

Our towns were shaken of tall kings
  With scarlet beards like blood;
The world turned empty where they trod,
They took the kindly cross of God
  And cut it up for wood.

Their souls were drifting as the sea,
  And all good towns and lands
They only saw with heavy eyes,
  And broke with heavy hands.

Their gods were sadder than the sea,
  Gods of a wandering will,
Who cried for blood like beasts at night,
  Sadly, from hill to hill.

They seemed as trees walking the earth,
  As witless and as tall,
Yet they took hold upon the heavens
  And no help came at all.

They bred like birds in English woods,
  They rooted like the rose,
When Alfred came to Athelney
  To hide him from their bows.

There was not English armour left,
  Nor any English thing,
When Alfred came to Athelney
  To be an English king.

For earthquake swallowing earthquake
  Uprent the Wessex tree;
The whirlpool of the pagan sway
Had swirled his sire, as sticks, away,
  When a flood smites the sea.

And the great kings of Wessex
  Wearied and sank in gore,
And even their ghosts in that great stress
Grew greyer and greyer, less and less,
With the lords that died in Lyonesse
  And the king that comes no more.

And the God of the Golden Dragon
  Was dumb upon his throne,
And the lord of the Golden Dragon
  Ran in the woods alone.

And if ever he climbed the crest of luck
  And set the flag before,
Returning, as a wheel returns,
Came ruin and the rain that burns,
  And all began once more.

THE VISION OF THE KING

And naught was left King Alfred
  But shameful tears of rage,
In the island in the river
  In the end of all his age.

In the island in the river
  He was broken to his knee;
And read, writ with an iron pen,
That God had wearied of Wessex men
And given their country, field and fen,
  To the devils of the sea.

And he saw in a little picture,
  Tiny and far away,
His mother, sitting in Egbert's hall,
And a book she showed him, very small,
Where a sapphire Mary sat in stall
  With a golden Christ at play.

It was wrought in the monk's slow manner,
  From silver and sanguine shell,
Where the scenes are little and terrible,
  Key-holes of heaven and hell.

In the river island of Athelney,
  With the river running past,
In colours of such simple creed
All things sprang at him, sun and weed,

Till the grass grew to be grass indeed
And the tree was a tree at last.

Fearfully plain the flowers grew,
    Like the child's book to read,
Or like a friend's face seen in a glass;
He looked; and there Our Lady was,
She stood and stroked the tall live grass
    As a man strokes his steed.

Her face was like an open word
    When brave men speak and choose,
The very colours of her coat
    Were better than good news.

She spoke not, nor turned not,
    Nor any sign she cast,
Only she stood up straight and free,
Between the flowers in Athelney,
    And the river running past.

One dim ancestral jewel hung
    On his ruined armour grey,
He rent and cast it at her feet:
Where, after centuries, with slow feet,
Men came from hall and school and street
    And found it where it lay.

THE VISION OF THE KING

"Mother of God," the wanderer said,
  "I am but a common king,
Nor will I ask what saints may ask,
  To see a secret thing.

"The gates of heaven are fearful gates,
  Worse than the gates of hell;
Not I would break the splendours barred,
Or seek to know what thing they guard,
  Which is too good to tell.

"But for this earth most pitiful,
  This little land I know,
If that which is forever is,
Or if our hearts shall break with bliss,
  Seeing the stranger go?

"When our last bow is broken, Queen,
  And our last javelin cast
Under some sad, green evening sky,
Holding a ruined cross on high,
Under warm westland grass to lie,
  Shall we come home at last?"

And a voice came human but high up,
  Like a cottage climbed among
The clouds; or a serf of hut and croft
That sits by his hovel fire as oft,

But hears, on his old bare roof aloft,
  A belfry burst in song.

"The gates of heaven are lightly locked,
  We do not guard our gain,
The heaviest hind may easily
Come silently and suddenly
  Upon me in a lane.

"And any little maid that walks
  In good thoughts apart,
May break the guard of the Three Kings,
And see the dear and dreadful things
  I hid within my heart.

"The meanest man in grey fields gone
  Behind the set of sun, .
Heareth between star and other star,
Through the door of the darkness fallen ajar,
The council, eldest of things that are,
  The talk of the Three in One.

"The gates of heaven are lightly locked,
  We do not guard our gold;
Men may uproot where worlds begin,
Or read the name of the nameless sin;
But if he fail or if he win
  To no good man is told.

THE VISION OF THE KING

"The men of the East may spell the stars,
　　And times and triumphs mark,
But the men signed of the cross of Christ
　　Go gaily in the dark.

"The men of the East may search the scrolls
　　For sure fates and fame,
But the men that drink the blood of God
　　Go singing to their shame.

"The wise men know what wicked things
　　Are written on the sky,
They trim sad lamps, they touch sad strings,
Hearing the heavy purple wings,
Where the forgotten Seraph kings
　　Still plot how God shall die.

"The wise men know all evil things
　　Under the twisted trees,
Where the perverse in pleasure pine,
And men are weary of green wine
　　And sick of crimson seas.

"But you and all the kind of Christ
　　Are ignorant and brave,
And you have wars you hardly win
　　And souls you hardly save.

THE BALLAD OF THE WHITE HORSE

"I tell you naught for your comfort,
    Yea, naught for your desire,
Save that the sky grows darker yet
    And the sea rises higher.

"Night shall be thrice night over you,
    And heaven an iron cope.
Do you have joy without a cause,
    Yea, faith without a hope?"

Even as she spoke she was not,
    Nor any word said he;
He only heard, still as he stood
Under the old night's nodding hood,
The sea-folk breaking down the wood
    Like a high tide from sea.

He only heard the heathen men,
    Whose eyes are blue and bleak,
Singing about some cruel thing
Done by a great and smiling king
    In daylight on a deck.

He only heard the heathen men,
    Whose eyes are blue and blind,
Singing what shameful things are done
Between the sunlit sea and the sun
    When the land is left behind.

BOOK II
THE GATHERING OF THE CHIEFS

THE GATHERING OF THE CHIEFS

Up over windy wastes and up
Went Alfred over the shaws,
Shaken of the joy of giants,
The joy without a cause.

In the slopes away to the western bays,
Where blows not ever a tree,
He washed his soul in the west wind
And his body in the sea.

And he set to rhyme his ale-measures
And he sang aloud his laws;
Because of the joy of the giants,
The joy without a cause.

For the King went gathering Wessex men
As grain out of the chaff;
The few that were alive to die,
Laughing, as littered skulls that lie
After lost battles turn to the sky
An everlasting laugh.

17

The King went gathering Christian men
  As wheat out of the husk;
Eldred the Franklin by the sea,
And Mark, the man from Italy,
And Golan of the Sacred Tree,
  From the old tribe on Usk.

The rook croaked homeward heavily,
  The west was clear and warm,
The smoke of evening food and ease
Rose like a blue tree in the trees
  When he came to Eldred's farm.

But Eldred's farm was fallen awry,
  Like an old cripple's bones,
And Eldred's tools were red with rust;
And on his well was a green crust,
And purple thistles upward thrust
  Between the kitchen stones.

But smoke of some good feasting
  Went upwards evermore;
And Eldred's doors stood wide apart
For loitering foot or labouring cart;
And Eldred's great and foolish heart
  Stood open, like his door.

A mighty man was Eldred;
  A bulk for casks to fill;

His face a dreaming furnace,
  His body a walking hill.

In the old wars of Wessex
  His sword had sunken deep,
But all his friends, he sighed and said,
Were broken about Ethelred;
And between the deep drink and the dead
  He had fallen upon sleep.

"Come not to me, King Alfred,
  Save always for the ale;
Why should my harmless hinds be slain
Because the chiefs cry once again,
As in all fights, that we shall gain,
  And in all fights we fail.

"Your scalds still thunder and prophesy
  That crown that never comes;
Friend, I will watch the certain things,
Swine, and slow moons like silver rings,
  And the ripening of the plums."

And Alfred answered, drinking,
  And gravely, without blame,
"Nor bear I boast of scald or king;
The thing I bear is a lesser thing,
  But comes in a better name.

19

"Out of the mouth of the Mother of God,
  More than the doors of doom,
I call the muster of Wessex men;
From grassy hamlet or ditch or den,
To break and be broken, God knows when,
  But I have seen for whom.

"Out of the mouth of the Mother of God
  Like a little word come I;
For I go gathering Christian men
From sunken paving and ford and fen,
To die in a battle, God knows when,
  By God, but I know why.

"And this is the word of Mary,
  The word of the world's desire,
'No more of comfort shall ye get,
Save that the sky grows darker yet
  And the sea rises higher.'"

Then silence sank. And slowly
  Arose the sea-land lord
Like some vast beast for mystery,
He filled the room and porch and sky,
And from a cobwebbed nail on high
  Unhooked his heavy sword.

Up on the shrill sea-downs and up
  Went Alfred, all alone,

THE GATHERING OF THE CHIEFS

And turned but once e'er the door was shut,
Shouting to Eldred over his butt
That he bring all spears to the woodman's hut
  Hewn under Egbert's Stone.

And he turned his back and broke the fern
  And fought the moths of dusk;
And went on his way for other friends —
Friends fallen of all the wide world's ends;
From Rome that wrath and pardon sends
  And the gray towns on Usk.

He saw gigantic tracks of death
  And many a shape of doom,
Good steadings to grey ashes gone
And a monk's house, white like a skeleton,
  In the green crypt of the combe.

And in many a Roman villa
  Earth and her ivies eat,
Saw coloured pavements sink and fade
In flowers; and the windy colonnade
  Like the spectre of a street.

But the cold stars clustered
  Among the cold pines
Ere he was half on his pilgrimage
  Over the western lines.

And the white dawn widened
    Ere he came to the last pine
Where Mark, the man from Italy,
    Still made the Christian sign.

The long farm lay on the large hill-side,
    Flat, like a painted plan,
And by the side the low white house
    Where dwelt the southland man.

A bronzed man, with a bird's bright eye
    And a strong bird's beak and brow;
His skin was brown like buried gold,
And of certain of his sires was told
That they came in the shining ship of old
    With Cæsar in the prow.

His fruit trees stood like soldiers,
    Drilled in a straight line;
His strange stiff olives did not fail,
And all the kings of the earth drank ale,
    But he drank wine.

Wide over wasted British plains
    Stood never an arch or dome,
Only the trees to toss and reel,
The tribes to bicker, the beasts to squeal;
But the eyes in his head were strong like steel
    And his soul remembered Rome.

THE GATHERING OF THE CHIEFS

Then Alfred of the lonely spear
  Lifted his lion head;
And fronted with the Italian's eye
Asking him of his whence and why,
  King Alfred stood and said:

"I am that oft defeated King
  Whose failure fills the land,
Who fled before the Danes of old,
Who chaffered with the Danes with gold,
Who now upon the Wessex wold
  Hardly has feet to stand.

"But out of the mouth of the Mother of God
  I have seen the truth like fire;
This, that the sky grows darker yet
  And the sea rises higher."

Long looked the Roman on the land;
  The trees as golden crowns
Blazed, drenched with dawn and dew-empearled,
While faintlier coloured, freshlier curled,
The clouds from underneath the world
  Stood up over the downs.

"These vines be ropes that drag me hard,"
  He said; "I go not far.
Where would you meet? For you must hold
Half Wiltshire and the White Horse wold

And the Thames bank to Owsenfold
    If Wessex goes to war.

"Guthrum sits strong on either bank,
    And you must press his lines
Inwards, and eastward drive him down;
I doubt if you shall take the crown
Till you have taken London town,
    For me, I have the vines."

"If each man on the Judgment Day
    Meet God on a plain alone,"
Said Alfred, "I will speak for you
As for myself, and call it true
That you brought all fighting folk you knew,
    Lined under Egbert's Stone.

"Though I be in the dust ere then
    I know where you will be."
And, shouldering suddenly his spear,
He faded like some elfin fear,
Where the tall pines ran up, tier on tier,
    Tree over toppling tree.

He shouldered his spear at morning,
    And laughed to lay it on,
But he leaned on his spear as on a staff,
With might and little mood to laugh,
Or ever he sighted chick or calf
    Of Colan of Caerleon.

THE GATHERING OF THE CHIEFS

For the man dwelt in a lost land
  Of boulders and broken men,
In a great grey cave far off to south,
Where a thick green forest stopped the mouth,
  Giving darkness in his den.

And the man was come like a shadow
  From the shadow of Druid trees,
Where Usk, with mighty murmurings,
Past Caerleon of the fallen kings,
  Goes out to ghostly seas.

Last of a race in ruin —
  He spoke the speech of the Gaels;
His kin were in holy Ireland
  Or up in the crags of Wales.

But his soul stood with his mother's folk,
  That were of the rain-wrapped isle
Where Patrick and Brandan westerly
Looked out at last on a landless sea
  And the sun's last smile.

His harp was carved and cunning
  As the Celtic craftsman makes,
Graven all over with twisting shapes
  Like many headless snakes.

His harp was carved and cunning,
His sword prompt and sharp,
And he was gay when he held the sword,
Sad when he held the harp.

For the great Gaels of Ireland
Are the men that God made mad,
For all their wars are merry
And all their songs are sad.

He kept the Roman order;
He made the Christian sign;
But his eyes grew often blind and bright,
And the sea that rose in the rocks at night
Rose to his head like wine.

He made the sign of the cross of God,
He knew the Roman prayer;
But he had unreason in his heart
Because of the gods that were.

Even they that walked on the high cliffs,
High as the clouds were then,
Gods of unbearable beauty
That broke the hearts of men.

And whether in seat or saddle,
Whether with frown or smile,
Whether at feast or fight was he,

He heard the noise of a nameless sea
  On an undiscovered isle.

Lifting the great green ivy,
And the great spear lowering,
One said, "I am Alfred of Wessex,
And I am a conquered king."

And the man of the cave made answer,
  And his eyes were stars of scorn,
"And better kings were conquered
  Or ever your sires were born.

"What goddess was your mother,
  What fay your breed begot,
That you should not die with Uther
  And Arthur and Lancelot?

"But when you win you brag and blow,
  And when you lose you rail,
Army of eastland yokels
  Not strong enough to fail."

"I bring not boast or railing,"
  Spake Alfred, not in ire;
"I bring of Our Lady a lesson set,
This — that the sky grows darker yet
  And the sea rises higher."

27

Then Colan of the Sacred Tree
  Tossed his black mane on high,
And cried, as rigidly he rose,
"And if the sea and sky be foes
  We will tame the sea and sky."

Smiled Alfred, "Seek ye a fable
  More dizzy and more dread
Than all your mad barbarian tales,
  Where the sky stands on its head?

"A tale where a man looks down on the sky
  That has long looked down on him;
A tale where a man can swallow a sea
  That might swallow the seraphim.

"Bring to the hut by Egbert's Stone
  All bills and bows ye have."
And Alfred strode off rapidly,
And Colan of the Sacred Tree
  Went slowly to his cave.

BOOK III
THE HARP OF ALFRED

THE HARP OF ALFRED

In a tree that yawned and twisted
  The King's few goods were flung,
A mass-book mildewed line by line,
And weapons and a skin of wine,
  And an old harp unstrung.

By the yawning tree in the twilight
  The King unbound his sword.
Severed the harp of all his goods,
And there in the cool and soundless woods
  Sounded a single chord.

Then laughed, and watched the finches flash,
  The sullen flies in swarm,
And went unarmed over the hills,
  With the harp upon his arm,

Until he came to the White Horse Vale
  And saw across the plains,
In the twilight high and far and fell,
Like the fiery terraces of hell,
  The camp fires of the Danes —

THE BALLAD OF THE WHITE HORSE

The fires of the Great Army
    That was made of iron men;
Whose fires of sacrilege and scorn
Ran around England red as morn;
Fires over Glastonbury Thorn —
    Fires out on Ely Fen.

And as he went by White Horse Vale
    He saw lie wan and wide
The old horse graven, God knows when,
By gods or beasts or what things then
Walked a new world instead of men,
    And scrawled on the hill-side.

And when he came to White Horse Down
    The great white horse was grey,
For it was ill scoured of the weed;
And lichen and thorn could crawl and feed
Since the foes of settled house and creed
    Had swept old works away.

King Alfred gazed all sorrowful
    At thistle and mosses grey,
Till a rally of Danes with shield and bill
Rolled drunk over the dome of the hill,
And, hearing of his harp and skill,
    They dragged him to their play.

THE HARP OF ALFRED

And as they went through the high green grass
  They roared like the great green sea;
But when they came to the red camp fire
  They were silent suddenly.

And as they went up the wastes away
  They went reeling to and fro;
But when they came to the red camp fire
  They stood all in a row.

For golden in the firelight,
  With a smile carved on his lips,
And a beard curled right cunningly,
Was Guthrum of the Northern Sea,
  The emperor of the ships —

With three great earls King Guthrum
  Went the rounds from fire to fire,
With Harold, nephew of the King,
And Ogier of the Stone and Sling,
And Elf, whose gold lute had a string
  That sighed like all desire.

The Earls of the Great Army
  That no men born could tire;
Whose flames anear him or aloof
Took hold of towers or walls of proof,
Fire over Glastonbury roof
  And out on Ely, fire.

And Guthrum heard the soldiers' tale
  And bade the stranger play;
Not harshly, but as one on high,
On a marble pillar in the sky,
Who sees all folks that live and die —
  Pigmy and far away.

And Alfred, King of Wessex,
  Looked on his conqueror —
And his hands hardened; but he played;
And leaving all later hates unsaid,
He sang of some old British raid
  On the wild west march of yore.

He sang of war in the warm wet shires
  Where rain nor fruitage fails,
Where England of the motley states
Deepens like a garden to the gates
  In the purple walls of Wales.

He sang of the seas of savage beads,
  And the seas and seas of spears
Boiling all over Offa's Dyke;
What time a Wessex club could strike
  The kings of the mountaineers.

Till Harold laughed and snatched the harp,
  The kinsman of the king,

THE HARP OF ALFRED

A big youth, beardless like a child,
Whom the new wine of war sent wild,
  Smote, and began to sing.

And he cried of the ships as eagles
  That circle fiercely and fly
And sweep the seas and strike the towns
  From Cyprus round to Skye.

Now swiftly and with peril
  They gather all good things,
The high horns of the forest beasts
  Or the secret stones of Kings.

"For Rome was given to rule the world,
  And gat of it little joy —
But we, but we shall enjoy the world,
  The whole huge world a toy.

"Great wine like blood from Burgundy,
  Cloaks like the clouds from Tyre,
And marble like solid moonlight
  And gold like frozen fire.

"Smells that a man might swill in a cup,
  Stones that a man might eat,
And the great smooth women like ivory
  That the Turks sell in the street."

He sang the throne of the thief of the world
  And the gods that love the thief;
And he yelled aloud at the cloister-yards
  Where men go gathering grief.

"Well have you sung, O stranger,
  Of death on the dyke in Wales,
Your chief was a bracelet-giver;
But the red unbroken river
Of a race runs not forever,
  But suddenly it fails.

"Doubtless your sires were sword-swingers
  When they waded fresh from foam,
Before they were turned to women
  By the god of the nails from Rome;

"But since you bent to the shaven men,
  Who neither lust nor smite,
Thunder of Thor, we hunt you
  A hare on the mountain height."

King Guthrum smiled a little,
  And said, "It is enough,
Nephew, let Elf retune the string;
A boy must needs like bellowing,
But the old ears of a careful King
  Are glad of songs less rough."

THE HARP OF ALFRED

Blue-eyed was Elf the minstrel,
  With womanish hair and ring,
Yet heavy was his hand on sword
  Though light upon the string.

And as he stirred the strings of the harp
  To notes but four or five,
The heart of each man moved in him
  Like a babe buried alive.

And they felt the land of the folk-songs
  Spread southward of the Dane,
And they heard the good Rhine flowing
  In the heart of all Allemagne.

They felt the land of the folk-songs,
  Where the gifts hang on the tree,
Where the girls give ale at morning
  And the tears come easily.

The mighty people, womanlike,
  That have pleasure in their pain,
As he sang of Balder beautiful,
  Whom the heavens loved in vain.

As he sang of Balder beautiful,
  Whom the heavens could not save,
Till the world was like a sea of tears
  And every soul a wave.

"There is always a thing forgotten
  When all the world goes well;
A thing forgotten, as long ago
When the gods forgot the mistletce;
And soundless as an arrow of snow,
  The arrow of anguish fell.

"The thing on the blind side of the heart,
  On the wrong side of the door,
The green plant groweth, menacing
Almighty lovers in the spring;
There is always a forgotten thing
  And love is not secure."

And all that sat by the fire were sad,
  Save Ogier, who was stern,
And his eyes hardened even to stones,
  As he took the harp in turn.

Earl Ogier of the Stone and Sling
  Was odd to ear and sight,
Old he was, but his locks were red,
And jests were all the words he said,
Yet he was sad at board and bed
  And savage in the fight.

"You sing of the young gods easily
  In the days when you are young;

But I must go smelling yew and sods,
And I know there are gods behind the gods,
  Gods that are best unsung.

"And a man grows ugly for women,
  And a man grows dull with ale;
Well if he find in his soul at last
  Fury that does not fail.

"The wrath of the gods behind the gods
  Who would rend all gods and men;
Well if the old man's heart hath still
Wheels sped of rage and roaring will
Like cataracts to break down and kill,
  Well for the old man then—

"While there is one tall shrine to shake
  Or one live man to rend;
For the wrath of the gods behind the gods
  Who are weary to make an end.

"There lives one moment for a man
  When the door at his shoulder shakes,
When the taut rope parts under the pull,
And the barest branch is beautiful
  One moment, while it breaks.

"So rides my soul upon the sea
  That drinks the howling ships;

Though in black jest it bows and nods
Under the moons with silver rods,
I know it is roaring at the gods,
　　Waiting the last eclipse.

"And in the last eclipse, the sea
　　Shall stand up like a tower,
Above all moons made dark and riven
Hold up its foaming head in heaven
　　And laugh, knowing its hour.

"And the high ones in the happy town
　　Propped by the planets seven,
Shall know a new light in the mind,
A noise about them and behind;
Shall hear an awful voice, and find
　　Foam in the courts of heaven.

"And you that sit by the fire are young
　　And true loves wait for you;
But the King and I grow old, grow old,
　　And hate alone is true."

And Guthrum shook his head but smiled,
　　For he was a mighty clerk,
And had read lines in the Latin books
　　When all the north was dark.

THE HARP OF ALFRED

He said, "I am older than you, Ogier;
    Not all things would I rend,
For whether life be bad or good,
    It is best to abide the end."

He took the great harp wearily,
    Even Guthrum of the Danes,
With wide eyes bright as the one long day
    On the long polar plains.

For he sang of a wheel returning,
    And the mire trod back to mire,
And how red hells and golden heavens
    Are castles in the fire.

"It is good to sit where the good tales go,
    To sit as our fathers sat;
But the hour shall come after his youth,
When a man shall know not tales but truth,
    And his heart fail thereat.

"When he shall read what is written
    So plain in clouds and clods,
When he shall hunger without hope
    Even for evil gods.

"For this is a heavy matter,
    And the truth is cold to tell;

Do we not know, have we not heard,
The soul is like a lost bird,
  The body a broken shell?

"And a man hopes, being ignorant,
  Till in white woods apart,
He finds at last the lost bird dead:
And a man may still lift up his head,
  But never more his heart.

"There comes no noise but weeping
  Out of the ancient sky,
And a tear is in the tiniest flower,
  Because the gods must die.

"The little brooks are very sweet
  Like a girl's ribbons curled,
But the great sea is bitter
  That washes all the world.

"Strong are the Roman roses
  Or the free flowers of the heath,
But every flower, like a flower of the sea,
  Smelleth with the salt of death.

"And the heart of the locked battle
  Is the happiest place for men;
When shrieking souls as shafts go by
And many have died and all may die;

Though this word be a mystery,
   Death is most distant then.

"Death blazes bright above the cup,
   And clear above the crown;
But in that dream of battle
   We seem to tread it down.

"Wherefore I am a great King
   And waste the world in vain,
Because man hath not other power,
Save that in dealing death for dower,
He may forget it for an hour
   To remember it again."

And slowly his hands and thoughtfully
   Fell from the lifted lyre,
And the owls moaned from the mighty trees
Till Alfred caught it to his knees
   And smote it as in ire.

He heaved the head of the harp on high,
   And swept the frame-work barred,
And his stroke had all the rattle and spark
   Of horses flying hard.

"When God put man in a garden
   He girt him with a sword,
And sent him forth a free knight,
   That might betray his lord;

"He brake Him and betrayed Him
  And fast and far he fell
Till you and I may stretch our necks
  And burn our beards in hell.

"But though I lie on the floor of the world
  With the seven sins for rods,
I would rather fall with Adam
  Than rise with all your gods.

"What have the strong gods given?
  Where have the glad gods led?
When Guthrum sits on a hero's throne
  And asks if he is dead?

"Sirs, I am but a nameless man,
  A rhymester without home,
Yet since I come to the Wessex clay
  And carry the cross of Rome,

"I will even answer the mighty earl
  That asked of Wessex men
Why they be meek and monkish folk,
And bow to the White Lord's broken yoke;
What sign have we save blood and smoke?
  Here is my answer then.

"That on you is fallen the shadow,
  And not upon the Name;

44

THE HARP OF ALFRED

That though we scatter and though we fly
And you hang over us like the sky
You are more tired of victory,
  Than we are tired of shame.

"That though you hunt the Christian man
  Like a hare in the hill-side
The hare has still more heart to run
  Than you have heart to ride.

"That though all lances split on you,
  All swords be heaved in vain,
We have more lust again to lose
  Than you to win again.

"Your lord sits high in the saddle,
  A broken-hearted king,
But our King Alfred, lost from fame,
Fallen among foes or bonds of shame,
In I know not what mean trade or name,
  Has still some song to sing;

"Our monks go robed in rain and snow
  But the heart of flame therein,
But you go clothed in feasts and flames
  When all is ice within;

45

ɒr shall all iron dooms make dumb
    ᴍen wondering ceaselessly,
If it be not better to fast for joy
    Than feast for misery.

"Nor monkish order only
    Slides down, as field to fen,
All things achieved and chosen pass
As the White Horse fades in the grass,
    No work of Christian men.

"Ere the sad gods that made your gods
    Saw their sad sunrise pass,
The White Horse of the White Horse Vale,
That you have left to darken and fail,
    Was cut out of the grass.

"Therefore your end is on you,
    Is on you and your kings,
Not for a fire in Ely fen,
Not that your gods are nine or ten,
But because it is only Christian men
    Guard even heathen things,

"For our God hath blessed creation,
    Calling it good. I know —
What spirit with whom you blindly band
Hath blessed destruction with this hand;

THE HARP OF ALFRED

But by God's death the stars shall sta
And the small apples grow."

And the King, with harp on shoulder,
  Stood up and ceased his song;
And the owls moaned from the mighty trees,
  And the Danes laughed loud and long.

BOOK IV
THE WOMAN IN THE FOREST

THE WOMAN IN THE FOREST

THE thunder of the snorting swine,
   Enormous in the gloam,
Rending among all roots that cling
And the wild horses whinnying
Were the night's noises when the King,
   Shouldering his harp, went home.

With eyes of owl and feet of fox,
   Full of all thoughts he went;
He marked the tilt of the pagan camp,
The paling of pine, the sentries' tramp,
And the one great stolen altar-lamp
   Over Guthrum in his tent.

By scrub and thorn in Ethandune
   That night the foe had lain;
Whence ran across the heather grey
The old stones of a Roman way;
And in a wood not far away
   The pale road split in twain.

He marked the wood and the cloven ways
   With an old captain's eyes,

And he thought how many a time had he
Sought to see Doom he could not see,
How ruin had come and victory
   And both were a surprise.

Even as he had watched and wondered,
   Under Ashdown from the plains;
With Ethelred praying in his tent,
Till the white hawthorn swung and bent
As Alfred rushed his spears and rent
   The shield-wall of the Danes.

Even so he had watched and wondered,
   Knowing neither less nor more,
Till all his lords lay dying
And axes on axes plying,
Flung him, and drove him flying
   Like a pirate to the shore.

Wise he had been before defeat,
   And wise before success;
Wise in both hours, and ignorant,
   Knowing neither more nor less.

As he went down to the river-hut
   He knew a night-shade scent,
Owls did as evil cherubs rise,

THE WOMAN IN THE FOREST

With little wings and lantern eyes,
As though he sank through the under-skies;
  But down and down he went.

As he went down to the river-hut
  He went as one that fell;
Seeing the high forest domes and spars
Dim green or torn with golden scars,
As the proud look up at the evil stars,
  In the red heavens of hell.

For he must meet by the river-hut
  Them he had bidden to arm,
Mark from the towers of Italy
And Colan of the Sacred Tree,
And Eldred who beside the sea
  Held heavily his farm.

The roof leaned gaping to the grass,
  As a monstrous mushroom lies;
Echoing and empty seemed the place;
But opened in a little space
A great grey woman, with scarred face
  And strong and humbled eyes.

King Alfred was but a meagre man,
  Bright eyed, but lean and pale;

And swordless with his harp and rags,
He seemed a beggar, such as lags
    Looking for crusts and ale.

And the woman, with a woman's eyes
    Of pity at once and ire,
Said, when that she had glared a span,
"There is a cake for any man
    If he will watch the fire."

And Alfred, bowing heavily,
    Sat down the fire to stir,
And even as the woman pitied him
    So did he pity her;

Saying, "O great heart in the night,
    O best cast forth for worst,
Twilight shall melt and morning stir,
And no kind thing shall come to her,
Till God shall turn the world over
    And all the last are first.

"And well may God with the serving-folk
    Cast in His dreadful lot;
Is not He too a servant
    And is not He forgot?

THE WOMAN IN THE FOREST

"For was not God my gardener
  And silent like a slave;
That opened oaks on the uplands
  Or thicket in graveyard gave?

"And was not God my armourer,
  All patient and unpaid,
That sealed my skull as a helmet
  And ribs for hauberk made?

"Did not a great grey servant
  Of all my sires and me,
Build this pavilion of the pines,
And herd the fowls and fill the vines,
And labour and pass and leave no signs
  Save mercy and mystery?

"For God is a great servant
  And rose before the day,
From some primordial slumber torn;
But all things living later born
Sleep on, and rise after the morn,
  And the Lord has gone away.

"On things half sprung from sleeping,
  All sleepy suns have shone;
They stretch stiff arms, the yawning trees,
The beasts blink upon hands and knees,

Man is awake and does and sees—
  But Heaven has done and gone.

"For who shall guess the good riddle
  Or speak of the Holiest,
Save in faint figures and failing words,
Who loves, yet laughs among the swords,
  Labours and is at rest?

"But some see God like Guthrum
  Crowned, with a great beard curled,
But I see God like a good giant,
  That, labouring, lifts the world.

"Wherefore was God in Golgotha,
  Slain as a serf is slain;
And hate He had of prince and peer,
And love He had and made good cheer
Of them that, like this woman here,
  Go powerfully in pain.

"But in this grey morn of man's life
  Cometh sometime to the mind
A little light that leaps and flies,
  Like a star blown on the wind.

"A star of nowhere, a nameless star,
  A light that spins and swirls,

THE WOMAN IN THE FOREST

And cries that even in hedge and hill,
Even on earth, it may go ill
   At last, with the evil earls.

"A dancing sparkle, a doubtful star,
   On the waste wind whirled and driven,
But it seems to sing of a wilder worth,
A time discrowned of doom and birth,
And the kingdom of the poor on earth
   Come, as it is in heaven.

"But, even though such days endure
   How shall it profit her?
Who shall go groaning to the grave,
With many a meek and mighty slave,
Field-breaker and fisher on the wave,
   And woodman and waggoner.

"Bake ye the big world all again
   A cake with kinder leaven;
Yet these are sorry evermore —
Unless there be a little door,
   A little door in heaven."

And as he wept for the woman
   He let her business be,
And like his royal oath and rash
The good food fell upon the ash
   And blackened instantly.

THE BALLAD OF THE WHITE HORSE

Screaming, the woman caught a cake
  Yet burning from the bar,
And struck him suddenly on the face,
  Leaving a scarlet scar.

King Alfred stood up wordless,
  A man dead with surprise,
And torture stood and the evil things
That are in the childish hearts of kings
  An instant in his eyes.

And even as he stood and stared
  Drew round him in the dusk
Those friends creeping from far-off farms,
Marcus with all his slaves in arms,
And the strange spears hung with ancient charms
  Of Colan of the Usk.

With one whole farm marching afoot
  The trampled road resounds,
Farm-hands and farm-beasts blundering by
And jars of mead and stores of rye,
Where Eldred strode above his high
  And thunder-throated hounds;

And grey cattle and silver lowed
  Against the unlifted morn,
And straw clung to the spear-shafts tall,

THE WOMAN IN THE FOREST

And a boy went before them all
  Blowing a ram's horn.

As mocking such rude revelry,
  The dim clan of the Gael
Came like a bad king's burial-end,
With dismal robes that drop and rend
And demon pipes that wail —

In long, outlandish garments,
  Torn, though of antique worth,
With Druid beards and Druid spears,
As a resurrected race appears
  Out of an elder earth.

And though the King had called them forth
  And knew them for his own,
So still each eye was, like a gem,
So spectral hung each broidered hem
Grey carven men he fancied them,
  Hewn in an age of stone.

And the two wild peoples of the north
  Stood fronting in the gloam,
And heard and knew each in his mind
A third great sound upon the wind,
The living walls that hedge mankind,
  The walking walls of Rome.

Mark's were the mixed tribes of the west
  Of many a hue and strain,
Gurth, with rank hair like yellow grass;
And the Cornish fisher, Gorlias,
And Halmer, come from his first mass,
  Lately baptized, a Dane.

But like one man in armour
  Those hundreds trod the field,
From red Arabia to the Tyne
The earth had heard that marching-line,
Since the cry on the hill Capitoline,
  And the fall of the golden shield.

And the earth shook and the King stood still
  Under the greenwood bough,
And the smoking cake lay at his feet
  And the blow was on his brow.

Then Alfred laughed out suddenly,
  Like the thunder in the spring,
Till shook aloud the lintel-beams,
And the squirrels stirred in dusty dreams,
And the startled birds went up in streams,
  For the laughter of the King.

And the beasts of the earth and the birds looked
    down,
  In a wild solemnity,

THE WOMAN IN THE FOREST

On a stranger sight than a sylph or elf,
On a man laughing at himself
  Under the greenwood tree —

The giant laughter of Christian men
  That roars through a thousand tales,
Where greed is an ape and pride is an ass,
And Jack's away with his master's lass,
And the miser is banged with all his brass,
  The farmer with all his flails;

Tales that tumble and tales that trick,
  Yet end not all in scorning —
Of kings and clowns in a merry plight,
And the clock gone wrong and the world gone
    right,
That the mummers sing upon Christmas night
  And Christmas Day in the morning.

"Now here is a good warrant,"
  Cried Alfred, "by my sword;
For he that is struck for an ill servant
  Should be a kind lord. ·

"He that has been a servant
  Knows more than priests and kings,
But he that has been an ill servant,
  He knows all earthly things.

61

"Pride flings frail palaces at the sky,
  As a man flings up sand,
But the firm feet of humility
  Take hold of heavy land.

"Pride juggles with her toppling towers,
  They strike the sun and cease,
But the firm feet of humility
  They grip the ground like trees.

"He that hath failed in a little thing
  Hath a sign upon the brow;
And the Earls of the Great Army
  Have no such seal to show.

"The red print on my forehead
  Small flame for a red star,
In the van of the violent marching, then
When the sky is torn of the trumpets ten,
And the hands of the happy howling men
  Fling wide the gates of war,

"This blow that I return not
  Ten times will I return
On kings and earls of all degree,
And armies wide as empires be
Shall slide like landslips to the sea,
  If the red star burn.

THE WOMAN IN THE FOREST

"One man shall drive a hundred,
   As the dead kings drave;
Before me rocking hosts be riven,
And battering cohorts backwards driven,
For I am the first king known of heaven
   That has been struck like a slave.

"Up on the old white road, brothers,
   Up on the Roman walls!
For this is the night of the drawing of swords,
And the painted tower of the heathen hordes
Leans to our hammers, fires and cords,
   Leans a little and falls.

"Follow the star that lives and leaps,
   Follow the sword that sings,
For we go gathering heathen men,
A terrible harvest, ten by ten,
As the wrath of the last red autumn — then
   When Christ reaps down the kings.

"Follow a light that leaps and spins,
   Follow the fire unfurled!
For riseth up against realm and rod,
A thing forgotten, a thing down trod,
The last lost giant, even God,
   Is risen against the world."

THE BALLAD OF THE WHITE HORSE

Roaring they went o'er the Roman wall,
  And roaring up the lane,
Their torches tossed, a ladder of fire,
Higher their hymn was heard and higher,
More sweet for hate and for heart's desire.
And up in the northern scrub and brier
  They fell upon the Dane.

BOOK V

ETHANDUNE: THE FIRST STROKE

ETHANDUNE: THE FIRST STROKE

King Guthrum was a dread king,
  Like death out of the north;
Shrines without name or number
He rent and rolled as lumber,
From Chester to the Humber
  He drove his foemen forth.

The Roman villas heard him
  In the valley of the Thames,
Come over the hills roaring
Above their roofs, and pouring
On spire and stair and flooring
  Brimstone and pitch and flames.

Sheer o'er the great chalk uplands
  And the hill of the Horse went he,
Till high on Hampshire beacons
  He saw the southern sea.

High on the heights of Wessex
  He saw the southern brine,
And turned him to a conquered land,

And where the northern thornwoods stand
And the road parts on either hand,
    There came to him a sign.

King Guthrum was a war-chief,
    A wise man in the field,
And though he prospered well, and knew
How Alfred's folk were sad and few,
Not less with weighty care he drew
    Long lines for pike and shield.

King Guthrum lay on the upper land,
    On a single road at gaze,
And his foe must come with lean array,
Up on the left arm of the cloven way,
    To the meeting of the ways.

And long ere the noise of armour,
    An hour ere the break of light,
The woods awoke with crash and cry,
And the birds sprang clamouring harsh and high,
And the rabbits ran like an elves' army
    Ere Alfred came in sight.

The live wood came at Guthrum,
    On foot and claw and wing,
The nests were noisy overhead,
For Alfred and the star of red,

ETHANDUNE: THE FIRST STROKE

All life went forth, and the forest fled
  Before the face of the King.

But halted in the woodways
  Christ's few were grim and grey,
And each with a small, far, bird-like sight
Saw the high folly of the fight;
And though strange joys had grown in the night,
  Despair grew with the day.

And then white dawn crawled through the wood
  Like cold foam of a flood,
Then weakened every warrior's mood,
In hope though not in hardihood;
And each man sorrowed as he stood
  In the fashion of his blood.

For the Saxon Franklin sorrowed
  For the things that had been fair,
For the dear, dead women, crimson-clad,
And the great feasts and the friends he had;
But the Celtic prince's soul was sad
  For the things that never were.

In the eyes Italian all things
  But a black laughter died;
And Alfred flung his shield to earth
  And smote his breast and cried —

"I wronged a man to his slaying,
　And a woman to her shame,
And once I looked on a sworn maid
　That was wed to the Holy Name.

"And once I took my neighbour's wife,
　That was bound to an eastland man,
In the starkness of my evil youth,
　Before my griefs began.

"People, if you have any prayers,
　Say prayers for me;
And lay me under a Christian stone
In that lost land I thought my own,
To wait till the holy horn is blown,
　And all poor men are free."

Then Eldred of the idle farm
　Leaned on his ancient sword,
As fell his heavy words and few;
And his eyes were of such alien blue
As gleams where the Northman saileth new
　Into an unknown fiord.

"I was a fool and wasted ale —
　My slaves found it sweet;
I was a fool and wasted bread,
　And the birds had bread to eat.

ETHANDUNE: THE FIRST STROKE

"The kings go up and the kings go down,
  And who knows who shall rule?
Next night a king may starve or sleep,
But men and birds and beasts shall weep
  At the burial of a fool.

"O, drunkards in my cellar,
  Boys in my apple tree,
The world grows stern and strange and new,
And wise men shall govern you,
  And you shall weep for me.

"But yoke me my own oxen
  Down to my own farm;
My own dog will whine for me,
My own friends will bend the knee,
And the foes I slew openly
  Have never wished me harm."

And all were moved a little,
  But Colan stood apart,
Having first pity, and after
Hearing, like rat in rafter,
That little worm of laughter
  That eats the Irish heart.

And his grey-green eyes were cruel,
  And the smile of his mouth waxed hard,

And he said, "And when did Britain
 Become your burying-yard?

"Before the Roman lit the land,
 When schools and monks were none,
We reared such stones to the sun-god
 As might put out the sun.

"The tall trees of Britain
 We worshipped and were wise,
But you shall raid the whole land through
And never a tree shall talk to you,
Though every leaf is a tongue taught true
 And the forest is full of eyes.

"On one round hill to the seaward
 The trees grow tall and grey,
And the trees talk together
 When all men are away.

"O'er a few round hills forgotten
 The trees grow tall in rings,
And the trees talk together
 Of many pagan things.

"Yet I could lie and listen
 With a cross upon my clay,
And hear unhurt for ever
 What the trees of Britain say."

ETHANDUNE: THE FIRST STROKE

A proud man was the Roman,
    His speech a single one,
But his eyes were like an eagle's eyes
    That is staring at the sun.

"Dig for me where I die," he said,
    "If first or last I fall —
Dead on the fell at the first charge,
    Or dead by Wantage wall;

"Lift not my head from bloody ground,
    Bear not my body home,
For all the earth is Roman earth
    And I shall die in Rome."

Then Alfred, King of England,
    Bade blow the horns of war,
And flung the Golden Dragon out,
With crackle and acclaim and shout,
    Scrolled and aflame and far.

And under the Golden Dragon
    Went Wessex all along,
Past the sharp point of the cloven ways,
Out from the black wood into the blaze
    Of sun and steel and song.

And when they came to the open land
    They wheeled, deployed, and stood.

THE BALLAD OF THE WHITE HORSE

Midmost were Marcus and the King,
And Eldred on the right-hand wing,
And leftwards Colan darkling,
In the last shade of the wood.

But the Earls of the Great Army
Lay like a long half moon;
Ten poles before their palisades
With wide-winged helms and runic blades,
Red giants of an age of raids
In the thornland of Ethandune.

Midmost the saddles rose and swayed
And a stir of horses' manes,
Where Guthrum and a few rode high
On horses seized in victory;
But Ogier went on foot to die,
In the old way of the Danes.

Far to the King's right Elf the bard
Led on the western wing
With songs and spells that change the blood;
And on the King's left Harold stood,
The kinsman of the King.

Young Harold, coarse, with colours gay,
Smoking with oil and musk,
And the pleasant violence of the young,
Pushed through his people, giving tongue

ETHANDUNE: THE FIRST STROKE

Foewards, where, grey as cobwebs, hung
   The banners of the Usk.

But as he came before this line
   A little space along,
His beardless face broke into mirth,
And he cried, "What broken bits of earth
Are here? For what their clothes are worth
   I would sell them for a song."

For Colan was hung with raiment
   Tattered like autumn leaves,
And his men were all as thin as saints,
   And all as poor as thieves.

No bows nor slings nor bolts they bore,
   But bills and pikes ill-made,
And none but Colan bore a sword,
   And rusty was its blade

And Colan's eyes with mystery
   And iron laughter stirred,
And he spoke aloud, but lightly,
   Not labouring to be heard

"Oh, truly we be broken hearts,
   For that cause, it is said,
We light our candles to that Lord
   That broke himself for bread.

"But though we hold but bitterly
  What land the Saxon leaves,
Though Ireland be but a land of saints,
  And Wales a land of thieves,

"I say you yet shall weary,
  Of the working of your word,
That stricken spirits never strike
  Nor lean hands hold a sword.

"And if ever ye ride in Ireland,
  The jest may yet be said,
There is the land of broken hearts,
  And the land of broken heads."

Not less barbarian laughter
  Choked Harold like a flood,
"And shall I fight with scarecrows
  That am of Guthrum's blood?

"Meeting may be of war-men,
  Where the best war-man wins;
But all this carrion a man shoots
  Before the fight begins."

And stopping in his onward strides,
  He snatched a bow in scorn
From some mean slave, and bent it on

ETHANDUNE: THE FIRST STROKE

Colan, whose doom grew dark, and shone
Stars evil over Caerleon,
  In the place where he was born.

For Colan had not bow nor sling,
  On a lonely sword leaned he,
Like Arthur on Excalibur
  In the battle by the sea.

To his great gold earring Harold
  Tugged back the feathered tail
And swift had sprung the arrow,
  But swifter sprang the Gael.

Whirling the one sword round his head,
  A great wheel in the sun,
He sent it splendid through the sky
Flying before the shaft could fly —
It smote Earl Harold over the eye,
  And blood began to run.

Colan stood bare and weaponless
  Earl Harold, as in pain,
Strove for a smile, put hand to head,
Stumbled and suddenly fell dead;
And the small white daisies all waxed red
  With blood out of his brain.

And all at that marvel of the sword,
  Cast like a stone to slay,
Cried out. Said Alfred, "Who would see
Signs, must give all things. Verily
Man shall not taste of victory
  Till he throws his sword away."

Then Alfred, prince of England,
  And all the Christian earls
Unhooked their swords and held them up,
Each offered to Colan, like a cup
  Of chrysolite and pearls.

And the King said, "Do thou take my sword
  Who have done this deed of fire,
For this is the manner of Christian men,
Whether of steel or priestly pen,
That they cast their hearts out of their ken
  To get their hearts' desire.

"And whether ye swear a hive of monks
  Or one fair wife to friend,
This is the manner of Christian men,
  That their oath endures the end.

"For Love, our Lord, at the end of the world,
  Sits a red horse like a throne,
With a brazen helmet and an iron bow,
  But one arrow alone.

ETHANDUNE: THE FIRST STROKE

"Love with the shield of the Broken Heart
  Ever his bow doth bend
With a single shaft for a single prize,
And the ultimate bolt that parts and flies
Comes with a thunder of split skies,
  And a sound of souls that rend.

"So shall you earn a king's sword,
  Who cast your sword away."
And the King took with a random eye,
A rude axe from a hind hard by,
  And turned him to the fray.

For the swords of the Earls of Daneland
  Flamed round the fallen lord,
The first blood woke the trumpet-tune,
As in monk's rhyme or wizard's rune
Beginneth the Battle of Ethandune
  With the throwing of the sword.

BOOK VI

ETHANDUNE: THE SLAYING OF THE CHIEFS

ETHANDUNE: THE SLAYING OF THE CHIEFS

As the sea flooding the flat sands
  Flew on the sea-born horde,
The two hosts shocked with dust and din,
Left of the Latian paladin,
Clanged all Prince Harold's howling kin
  On Colan and the sword.

Crashed in the midst on Marcus,
  Ogier with Guthrum by,
And westward of such central stir,
Far to the right and faintlier
The house of Elf, the harp-player,
  Struck Eldred's with a cry.

The centre swat for weariness,
  Stemming the screaming horde,
And wearily went Colan's hands
  That swung King Alfred's sword.

But like a cloud of evening
  To westward easily

THE BALLAD OF THE WHITE HORSE

Tall Eldred broke the sea of spears
  As a tall ship breaks the sea.

His face like a sanguine sunset,
  His shoulder a Wessex down,
His hand like a windy hammer-stroke;
Men could not count the crests he broke,
  So fast the crests went down.

As the tall white devil of the Plague
  Moves out of Asian skies,
With his foot on a waste of cities
  And his head in a cloud of flies;

Or purple and peacock skies grow dark
  With a moving locust-tower;
Or tawny sand-winds tall and dry,
Like hell's red banners beat and fly,
When death comes out of Araby,
  Was Eldred in his hour.

But while he moved like a massacre
  He murmured as in sleep,
And his words were all of low hedges
  And little fields and sheep.

Even as he strode like a pestilence,
  That strides from Rhine to Rome,

He thought how tall his beans might be
If ever he went home.

Spoke some stiff piece of childish prayer,
Dull as the distant chimes,
That thanked our God for good eating
And corn and quiet times—

Till on the helm of a high chief
Fell shatteringly his brand,
And the helm broke and the bone broke
And the sword broke in his hand.

Then from the yelling Northmen
Driven splintering on him ran
Full seven spears, and the seventh
Was never made by man.

Seven spears, and the seventh
Was wrought as the faerie blades
And given to Elf the minstrel
By the monstrous water-maids;

By them that dwell where luridly
Lost waters of the Rhine
Move among roots of nations,
As if sunken for a sign.

Under all graves they murmur,
  They murmur and rebel,
Down to the buried kingdoms creep
And like a lost rain roar and weep
  O'er the red heavens of hell.

Thrice drowned was Elf the minstrel
  And washed as dead on sand;
And the third time men found him
  The spear was in his hand.

Seven spears went about Eldred,
  Like stays about a mast;
But there was sorrow by the sea
  For the driving of the last.

Six spears driven upon Eldred
  Were splintered while he laughed;
One spear thrust into Eldred
  Three feet of blade and shaft,

And from the great heart grievously
  Came forth the shaft and blade,
And he stood with the face of a dead man,
  Stood a little, and swayed —

Then fell, as falls a battle-tower,
  On smashed and struggling spears,
Cast down from some unconquered town
That, rushing earthward, carries down
Loads of live men of all renown—
  Archers and engineers.

And a great clamour of Christian men
  Went up in agony,
Crying, "Fallen is the tower of Wessex
  That stood beside the sea."

Centre and right the Wessex guard
  Grew pale for doubt and fear,
And the flank failed at the advance,
For the death-light on the wizard lanes —
  The star of the evil spear.

"Stand like an oak," cried Marcus,
  "Stand like a Roman wall!
Eldred the good is fallen—
  Are you too good to fall?

"When ye were wan and bloodless
  He gave you ale enow;
The pirates deal with him as dung;
  God! are you bloodless now?"

"Grip, Wulf and Gorlias, grip the ash!
    Slaves, and I make you free!
Stamp, Hildred, hard in English land,
Stand Gurth, stand Gorlias, Gawen stand!
Hold, Halfgar, with the other hand,
    Halmer, hold up on knee!

"The lamps are dying in your homes,
    The fruits upon your bough;
Even now your old thatch smoulders, Gurth;
Now is the judgment of the earth,
    Now is the death-grip, now!"

For thunder of the captain,
    Not less the Wessex line,
Leaned back and reeled a space to rear
As Elf charged with the Rhine maid's spear,
    And roaring like the Rhine.

For the men were born by the waving walls
    Of woods and clouds that pass,
By dizzy plain and drifting sea,
And they mixed God with glamoury,
God with the gods of the burning tree
    And the wizard's tower and glass.

But Mark was come of the glittering towns
    Where hot white details show,

ETHANDUNE: SLAYING OF CHIEFS

Where men can number and expound,
And his faith grew in a hard ground
Of doubt and reason and falsehood found,
  Where no faith else could grow.

Belief that grew of all beliefs
  A moment back was blown;
And belief that stood on unbelief
  Stood up iron and alone.

The Wessex crescent backwards
  Crushed, as with bloody spear
Went Elf roaring and routing,
And Mark against Elf yet shouting,
  Shocked, in his mid-career.

Right on the Roman shield and sword
  Did spear of the Rhine maids run;
But the shield shifted never,
The sword rang down to sever,
And the great Rhine sang forever,
  And the songs of Elf were done.

And a great thunder of Christian men
  Went up against the sky,
Saying, "God hath broken the evil spear
  Ere the good man's blood was dry."

"Spears at the charge!" yelled Mark amain.
  "Death on the gods of death!
Over the thrones of doom and blood
Goeth God that is a craftsman good,
And gold and iron, earth and wood,
  Loveth and laboureth.

"The fruits leap up in all your farms,
  The lamps in each abode;
God of all things done on earth,
All wheels or webs of any worth,
The God that makes the roof, Gurth,
  The God that makes the road.

"The God that heweth kings in oak,
  Writeth songs on vellum,
God of gold and flaming glass,
Confregit potentias
Arcuum scutum, Gorlias,
  Gladium et bellum."

Steel and lightning broke about him,
  Battle-bays and palm,
All the sea-kings swayed among
Woods of the Wessex arms upflung,
The trumpet of the Roman tongue,
  The thunder of the psalm.

And midmost of that rolling field
   Ran Ogier ragingly,
Lashing at Mark, who turned his blow,
And brake the helm about his brow
   And broke him to his knee.

Then Ogier heaved over his head
   His huge round shield of proof;
Then Mark set one foot on the shield,
One on some sundered rock upheeled,
And towered above the tossing field,
   A statue on a roof.

Dealing far blows about the fight,
   Like thunder-bolts a-roam,
Like birds about the battle-field,
While Ogier writhed under his shield
   Like a tortoise in his dome.

But hate in the buried Ogier
   Was strong as pain in hell,
With bare brute hand from the inside
He burst the shield of brass and hide,
And a death-stroke to the Roman's side
   Sent suddenly and well.

Then the great statue on the shield
   Looked his last look around

With level and imperial eye;
And Mark, the man from Italy,
Fell in the sea of agony,
　And died without a sound.

And Ogier, leaping up alive
　Hurled his huge shield away
Flying, as when a juggler flings
　A whizzing plate in play.

And held two arms up rigidly
　And roared to all the Danes:
"Fallen is Rome, yea, fallen
　The city of the plains! —

"Shall no man born remember,
　That breaketh wood or weald,
How long she stood on the roof of the world
　As he stood on my shield.

"The new wild world forgetteth her
　As foam fades on the sea,
How long she stood with her foot on Man
　As he with his foot on me.

"No more shall the brown men of the south
　Move like the ants in lines,

ETHANDUNE: SLAYING OF CHIEFS

To quiet men with olives
  Or madden men with vines.

"No more shall the white towns of the south
  Where Tiber and Nilus run,
Sitting around a secret sea
  Worship a secret sun.

"The blind gods roar for Rome fallen,
  And forum and garland gone,
For the ice of the north is broken,
  And the sea of the north comes on.

"The blind gods roar and rave and dream
  Of all cities under the sea,
For the heart of the north is broken,
  And the blood of the north is free.

"Down from the dome of the world we come,
  Rivers on rivers down,
Under us swirl the sects and hordes
  And the high dooms we drown.

" Down from the dome of the world and down
  Struck flying as a skiff
On a river in spate is spun and swirled
Until we come to the end of the world
  That breaks short, like a cliff.

THE BALLAD OF THE WHITE HORSE

"And when we come to the end of the world,
  For me, I count it fit
To take the leap like a good river,
  Shot shrieking over it.

"But whatso hap at the end of the world,
  Where Nothing is struck and sounds,
It is not, by Thor, these monkish men
  These humbled Wessex hounds—

"Not this pale line of Christian hinds,
  This one white string of men,
Shall keep us back from the end of the world,
  And the things that happen then.

"It is not Alfred's dwarfish sword,
  Nor Egbert's pigmy crown,
Shall slay us now that descend in thunder,
Rending the realms and the realms thereunder,
  Down through the world and down."

There was that in the wild men back of him,
  There was that in his own wild song,
A dizzy throbbing, a drunkard smoke,
That dazed to death all Wessex folk,
  And swept their spears along.

ETHANDUNE: SLAYING OF CHIEFS

Vainly the sword of Colan
  And the axe of Alfred plied—
The Danes poured in like a brainless plague,
  And knew not when they died.

Prince Colan slew a score of them,
  And was stricken to his knee;
King Alfred slew a score and seven,
  And was borne back on a tree.

Back to the black gate of the woods,
  Back up the single way,
Back by the place of the parting ways
  Christ's knights were whirled away.

And when they came to the parting ways
  Doom's heaviest hammer fell,
For the King was beaten, blind, at bay,
Down the right lane with his array.
But Colan swept the other way
  Where he smote great strokes and fell.

The thorn-woods over Ethandune
  Stand sharp and thick as spears;
By night and furze and forest-harms
Far sundered were the friends in arms;
The loud lost blows, the last alarms,
  Came not to Alfred's ears.

The thorn-woods over Ethandune
  Stand stiff as spikes in mail;
As to the Haut King came at morn
Dead Roland on a doubtful horn,
Seemed unto Alfred lightly borne
  The last cry of the Gael.

BOOK VII

ETHANDUNE: THE LAST CHARGE

ETHANDUNE: THE LAST CHARGE

Away in the waste of White Horse Down
  An idle child alone
Played some small game through hours that pass
And patiently would pluck the grass,
  Patiently push the stone.

On the lean, green edge for ever,
  Where the blank chalk touched the turf,
The child played on, alone, divine,
As a child plays on the last line
  That sunders sand and surf.

For he dwelleth in high divisions
  Too simple to understand,
Seeing on what morn of mystery
The Uncreated rent the sea
  With roarings from the land.

Through the long infant hours like days
  He built one tower in vain—
Piled up small stones to make a town,
And evermore the stones fell down,
  And he piled them up again.

And crimson kings on battle-towers,
  And saints on Gothic spires,
And hermits on their peaks of snow,
  And heroes on their pyres,

And patriots riding royally
  That rush the rocking town,
Stretch hands, and hunger and aspire,
Seeking to mount where high and higher,
The child whom Time can never tire,
  Sings over White Horse Down.

And this was the might of Alfred
  At the ending of the way;
That of such smiters wise or wild,
He was least distant from the child,
  Piling stones all day.

For Eldred fought like a frank hunter,
  That killeth and goeth home;
And Mark had fought because all arms
  Rang like the name of Rome.

And Colan fought with a double mind,
  Moody and madly gay;
But Alfred fought as gravely
  As a good child at play.

ETHANDUNE: THE LAST CHARGE

He saw wheels break and work run back,
  And all things as they were;
And his heart was orbed like victory,
  And simple like despair.

Therefore is Mark forgotten,
  That was wise with his tongue and brave;
And the cairn over Colan crumbled,
  And the cross on Eldred's grave.

Their great souls went on a wind away,
  And they have not tale or tomb;
And Alfred born in Wantage
  Rules England till the doom.

Because in the forest of all fears,
  Like a strange fresh gust from sea,
Struck him that ancient innocence
  That is more than mastery.

And as a child whose bricks fall down,
  Re-piles them o'er and o'er;
Came ruin and the rain that burns,
Returning as a wheel returns,
And crouching in the furze and ferns
  He began his life once more.

He took his ivory horn unslung
  And smiled, but not in scorn;
"Endeth the Battle of Ethandune
  With the blowing of a horn."

On a dark horse at the double way
  He saw great Guthrum ride;
Heard roar of brass and ring of steel,
The laughter and the trumpet peal,
  The pagan in his pride,

And Ogier's red and hated head
  Moved in some talk or task;
But the men seemed scattered in the brier,
And some of them had lit a fire,
  And one had broached a cask.

And waggons one or two stood up,
  Like tall ships in sight,
As if an outpost were encamped
  At the cloven ways for night.

And joyous of the sudden stay
  Of Alfred's routed few,
Sat one upon a stone to sigh;
And some slipped up the road to fly,
Till Alfred in the fern hard by
  Set horn to mouth and blew.

And they all abode like statues —
  One sitting on the stone,
One half-way through the thorn hedge tall,
One with a leg across a wall;
And one looked backwards, very small,
  Far up the road, alone.

Grey twilight and a yellow star
  Hung over thorn and hill.
Two spears and a cloven war-shield lay
Loose on the road as cast-away,
The horn died faint in the forests grey,
  And the fleeing men stood still.

"Brothers at arms," said Alfred,
  "On this side lies the foe;
Are slavery and starvation flowers
  That you should pluck them so?

"For whether is it better
  To be prodded with Danish poles,
Having hewn a chamber in a ditch,
And hounded like a howling witch,
  Or smoked to death in holes?

"Or that before the red cock crow,
  All we, a thousand strong,
Go down the dark road to God's house,
  Singing a Wessex song?

"To sweat a slave to a race of slaves,
　To drink up infamy?
No, brothers, by your leave, I think
Death is a better ale to drink;
And by all the stars of Christ that sink,
　The Danes shall drink with me.

"To grow old cowed in a conquered land,
　With the sun itself discrowned,
To see trees crouch and cattle slink —
Death is a better ale to drink,
And by high Death on the fell brink,
　That flagon shall go round.

"Though dead are all the paladins,
　Whom Glory had in ken,
Though all your thunder-sworded thanes
With proud hearts died among the Danes,
While a man remains, great war remains;
　Now is a war of men.

"The men that tear the furrows,
　The men that fell the trees;
When all their lords be lost and dead,
The bondsmen of the earth shall tread
　The tyrants of the seas.

"The wheel of the roaring stillness
　Of all labours under the sun,

Speed the wild work as well at least,
  As the whole world's work is done.

"Let Hildred hack the shield-wall,
  Clean as he hacks the hedge;
Let Gurth the Fowler stand as cool
  As he stands on the chasm's edge;

"Let Gorlias ride the sea-kings
  As Gorlias rides the sea,
Then let all hell and Denmark drive,
Yelling to all its fiends alive,
  And not a rag care we."

When Alfred's word was ended,
  Stood firm that feeble line,
Each in his place with club or spear,
And fury deeper than deep fear,
  And smiles as sour as brine.

And the King held up the horn and said,
  "See ye my father's horn,
That Egbert blew in his empery,
Once, when he rode out commonly,
Twice when he rode for venery,
  And thrice on the battle-morn.

"But heavier fates have fallen
  The horn of the Wessex kings;

And I blew once, the riding sign,
To call you to the fighting line
 And glory and all good things,

"And now two blasts, the hunting sign,
 Because we turn to bay;
But I will not blow the three blasts,
 Till we be lost or they.

"And now I blow the hunting sign,
 Charge some, by rule and rod,
But when I blow the battle sign,
 Charge all, and go to God."

Wild stared the Danes at the double ways
 Where they loitered, all at large,
As that dark line for the last time
 Doubled the knee to charge —

And caught their weapons clumsily,
 And marvelled how and why —
In such degree, by rule and rod,
The people of the peace of God
 Went roaring down to die.

And when the last arrow,
 Was fitted and was flown,
When the broken shield hung on the breast,

ETHANDUNE: THE LAST CHARGE

And the hopeless lance was laid in rest,
   And the hopeless horn blown,

The King looked up, and what he saw
   Was a great light like death,
For our Lady stood on the standards rent,
As lonely and as innocent
As when between white walls she went
   In the lilies of Nazareth.

One instant in a still light,
   He saw Our Lady then,
Her dress was soft as western sky,
And she was a queen most womanly —
   But she was a queen of men.

Over the iron forest
   He saw Our Lady stand;
Her eyes were sad withouten art,
And seven swords were in her heart —
   But one was in her hand.

Then the last charge went blindly,
   And all too lost for fear;
The Danes closed round, a roaring ring,
And twenty clubs rose o'er the King,
Four Danes hewed at him, halloing,
And Ogier of the Stone and Sling
   Drove at him with a spear.

But the Danes were wild with laughter,
And the great spear swung wide,
The point stuck to a straggling tree,
And either host cried suddenly,
As Alfred leapt aside.

Short time had shaggy Ogier
To pull his lance in line —
He knew King Alfred's axe on high,
He heard it rushing through the sky,

He cowered beneath it with a cry —
It split him to the spine;
And Alfred sprang over him dead,
And blew the battle sign.

Then bursting all and blasting,
Came Christendom like death,
Kicked from such catapults of will
The staves shiver, the barrels spill,
The waggons waver and crash and kill
The waggoners beneath.

Barriers go backwards, banners rend,
Great shields groan like a gong —
Horses like horns of nightmare
Neigh horribly and long.

ETHANDUNE: THE LAST CHARGE

Horses ramp high and rock and boil
  And break their golden reins,
And slide on carnage clamorously,
Down where the bitter blood doth lie,
Where Ogier went on foot to die,
  In the old way of the Danes.

"The high tide!" King Alfred cried;
  "The high tide and the turn!
As a tide turns on the tall grey seas,
See how they waver in the trees,
How stray their spears, how knock their knees,
  How wild their watchfires burn!

"The Mother of God goes over them,
  Walking on wind and flame,
And the storm-cloud drifts from city and dale,
And the White Horse stamps in the White Horse
    Vale,
And we all shall yet drink Christian ale,
  In the village of our name.

"The Mother of God goes over them,
  On dreadful Cherubs borne;
And the psalm is roaring above the rune,
And the cross goes over the sun and moon;
Endeth the Battle of Ethandune,
  With the blowing of the horn."

For back indeed disorderly
  The Danes went clamouring,
Too worn to take anew the tale,
Or dazed with insolence and ale,
Or stunned of heaven, or stricken pale
  Before the face of the King.

For dire was Alfred in his hour
  The pale scribe witnesseth,
More mighty in defeat was he
Than all men else in victory;
And behind, his men came murderously,
  Dry-throated, drinking death.

And Edgar of the Golden Ship
  He broke with his own hand,
Took Ludwig from his lady's bower,
And smote down Harmer in his hour,
And vain and lonely stood the tower —
  The tower in Guelderland.

And Torr out of his tiny boat,
  Whose eyes beheld the Nile,
Wulf with his war cry on his lips,
And Hacro born in the eclipse,
Who blocked the Seine with battle-ships
  Round Paris on the Isle.

ETHANDUNE: THE LAST CHARGE

And Hacon of the Harvest-song,
  And Dirck from the Elbe he slew,
And Cnut that melted Durham bell,
And Fulk and fiery Oscar fell,
And Goderic and Sigael,
  And Uriel of the Yew.

And highest sang the slaughter,
  And fastest fell the slain,
When from the wood-road's blackening throat
A crowning and crashing wonder smote
  The rear-guard of the Dane.

For the dregs of Colan's company —
  Lost down the other road,
Had gathered and grown and heard the din,
And with wild yells came pouring in
Naked as their old British kin
  And bright with blood for woad.

And bare and bloody and aloft
  They bore before their band
The body of their mighty lord,
Colan of Caerleon, and the horde,
That bore King Alfred's battle-sword
  Broken in his left hand.

And a strange music went with him,
  Loud and yet strangely far;

THE BALLAD OF THE WHITE HORSE

The wild pipes of the western land,
    Too keen for the ear to understand,
Sang high and deathly on each hand
    When the dead man went to war.

Blocked between ghost and buccaneer,
    Brave men have dropped and died,
And the wild sea-lords well might quail
As the ghastly war-pipes of the Gael
Called to the horns of White Horse Vale,
    And all the horns replied.

And Hildred the poor hedger
    Cut down four captains dead,
And Halfgar laid seven others low,
And the great earls wavered to and fro
    For the living and the dead.

And Gorlias grasped the great flag,
    The Raven of Odin, torn;
And the eyes of Guthrum altered,
    For the first time since morn.

As a turn of the wheel of tempest
    Tilts up the whole sky tall,
And cliffs of wan cloud luminous
Lean out like great walls over us,
    As if the heavens might fall;

ETHANDUNE: THE LAST CHARGE

As such a tall and tilted sky
  Sends certain snow or light,
So did the eyes of Guthrum change,
And the turn was more certain and more strange
  Than a thousand men in flight.

For not till the floor of the skies is split
  And hell-fire shines through the sea,
Or the stars look up through the rent earth's
    knees,
Cometh such rending of certainties,
As when one wise man truly sees
  What is more wise than he.

He set his horse in the battle-breach
  Even Guthrum of the Dane,
And as ever had fallen fell his brand,
A falling tower o'er many a land,
But Gurth the Fowler laid one hand
  Upon this bridle rein.

King Guthrum was a great lord,
  And higher than his gods —
He put the popes to laughter,
  He chid the saints with rods.

He took this hollow world of ours
  For a cup to hold his wine;

In the parting of the woodways
  There came to him a sign.

In Wessex in the forest,
  In the breaking of the spears,
We set a sign on Guthrum
  To blaze a thousand years.

Where the high saddles jostle
  And the horse-tails toss,
There rose to the birds flying
A roar of dead and dying;
In deafness and strong crying
  We signed him with the cross.

Far out to the winding river
  The blood ran down for days,
When we put the cross on Guthrum
  In the parting of the ways.

BOOK VIII
THE SCOURING OF THE HORSE

THE SCOURING OF THE HORSE

In the years of the peace of Wessex,
  When the good king sat at home;
Years following on that bloody boon
When she that stands above the moon
Stood above death at Ethandune,
  And saw his kingdom come —

When the pagan people of the sea
  Fled to their palisades,
Nailed there with javelins to cling,
And wonder smote the pirate king,
And brought him to his christening
  And the end of all his raids;

(For not till the night's blue slate is wiped
  Of its last star utterly,
And new strange signs writ there to read,
Shall eyes with such amazement heed
As when a great man knows indeed
  A greater thing than he.)

And there came to his chrism-loosing
  Lords of all lands afar;

And a line was drawn north-westerly,
That set King Egbert's empire free,
Giving all lands by the northern sea,
  To the sons of the northern star.

In the days of the rest of Alfred,
  When all these things were done,
And Wessex lay in a patch of peace,
  Like a dog in a patch of sun —

The King sat in his orchard,
  Among apples green and red,
With the little book in his bosom,
  And the sunshine on his head.

And he gathered the songs of simple men
  That swing with helm and hod,
And the alms he gave as a Christian
Like a river alive with fishes ran;
And he made gifts to a beggar man
  As to a wandering god.

And he gat good laws of the ancient kings,
  Like treasure out of the tombs;
And many a thief in thorny nook,
Or noble in sea-stained turret shook,
For the opening of his iron book,
  And the gathering of the dooms.

THE SCOURING OF THE HORSE

Then men would come from the ends of the earth
  Whom the King sat welcoming,
And men would go to the ends of the earth
  Because of the word of the King.

For folk came in to Alfred's face
  Whose javelins had been hurled
On monsters that make boil the sea,
Crakens and coils of mystery,
Or thrust in ancient snows that be
  The white hair of the world.

And some had knocked at the northern gates
  Of the ultimate icy floor,
Where the fish freeze and the foam turns black
And the wide world narrows to a track,
And the other sea at the world's back
  Cries through a closed door.

And men went forth from Alfred's face,
  Even great gift-bearing lords,
Not to Rome only, but more bold,
Out to the high hot courts of old,
Of negroes clad in cloth of gold,
  Silence, and crooked swords.

Scrawled screens and secret gardens
  And insect-laden skies —

Where fiery plains stretch on and on
To the purple country of Prester John
   And the walls of Paradise.

And he knew the might of the Terre Majeure,
   Where kings began to reign;
Where in a night-rout without name,
Of gloomy Goths and Gauls there came
White, above candles all aflame,
   Like a vision, Charlemagne.

And men, seeing such embassies,
   Spake with the King and said:
"The steel that sang so sweet a tune
On Ashdown and on Ethandune,
Why hangs it scabbarded so soon,
   All heavily like lead?

"Why dwell the Danes in North England,
   And up to the river ride?
Three more such marches like thine own
Would end them; and the Pict should own
Our sway; and our feet climb the throne
   In the mountains of Strathclyde."

And Alfred in the orchard,
   Among apples green and red,
With the little book in his bosom,
   Looked at green leaves and said:

THE SCOURING OF THE HORSE

"When all philosophies shall fail,
    This word alone shall fit;
That a sage feels too small for life,
    And a fool too large for it.

"Asia and all imperial plains
    Are too little for a fool;
But for one man whose eyes can see,
The little island of Athelney
    Is too large a land to rule.

"Haply it had been better
    When I built my fortress there,
Out in the reedy waters wide,
I had stood on my mud wall and cried:
'Take England all from tide to tide —
    Be Athelney my share.'

"Those madmen of the throne-scramble —
    Oppressors and oppressed —
Had lined the banks by Athelney,
And waved and wailed unceasingly,
Where the river turned to the broad sea,
    By an island of the blest.

"An island like a little book,
    Full of a hundred tales,
Like the gilt page the good monks pen,

That is all smaller than a wren,
Yet hath high towns, meteors and men,
And suns and spouting whales;

"A land having a light on it,
In the river dark and fast,
An isle with utter clearness lit,
Because a saint had stood in it;
Where flowers are flowers indeed and fit,
And trees are trees at last.

"So were the island of a saint;
But I am a common king,
And I will make my fences tough
From Wantage town to Plymouth Bluff,
Because I am not wise enough
To rule so small a thing."

And it fell in the days of Alfred,
In the days of his repose,
That as old customs in his sight,
Were a straight road and a steady light,
He bade them keep the White Horse white
As the first plume of the snows.

And right to the red torchlight,
From the trouble of morning grey,
They stripped the White Horse of the grass
As they strip it to this day.

THE SCOURING OF THE HORSE

And under the red torchlight
  He went dreaming as though dull
Of his old companions slain like kings,
And the rich irrevocable things
Of a heart that hath not openings,
  But is shut fast, being full.

And the torchlight touched the pale hair
  Where silver clouded gold,
And the frame of his face was made of cords;
And a young lord turned among the lords,
  And said, "The King is old."

And even as he said it,
  A post ran in amain,
Crying: "Arm, Lord King, the hamlets arm!
In the horror and the shade of harm,
They have burnt Brand of Aynger's farm —
  The Danes are come again!

"Danes drive the white East Angles
  In six fights on the plains;
Danes waste the world about the Thames,
Danes to the eastward — Danes!"

And as he stumbled on one knee,
  The thanes broke out in ire,
Crying, "Ill the watchmen watch, and ill
  The sheriffs keep the shire."

But the young earl said: "Ill the saints,
  The saints of England, guard
The land wherein we pledge them gold!
The dykes decay, the King grows old,
  And surely this is hard,

"That we be never rid of them,
  That when his head is hoar,
He cannot say to them he smote
And spared with a hand hard at the throat,
  'Go, and return no more.'"

Then Alfred smiled. And the smile of him
  Was like the sun for power.
But he only pointed; bade them heed
Those peasants of the Berkshire breed,
Who plucked the old Horse of the weed
  As they pluck it to this hour.

"Will ye part with the weeds for ever?
  Or show daisies to the door?
Or will you bid the bold grass
  Go, and return no more?

"So ceaseless and so secret,
  Thrive terror and theft set free;
Treason and shame shall come to pass
While one weed flowers in a morass;

THE SCOURING OF THE HORSE

And like the stillness of stiff grass
  The stillness of tyranny.

"Over our white souls also
  Wild heresies and high
Wave prouder than the plumes of grass,
  And sadder than their sigh.

"And I go riding against the raid,
  And ye know not where I am;
But ye shall know in a day or year,
When one green star of grass grows here;
Chaos has charged you, charger and spear,
  Battle-axe and battering-ram.

"And though skies alter and empires melt,
  This word shall still be true:
If we would have the horse of old,
  Scour ye the horse anew.

"One time I followed a dancing star
  That seemed to sing and nod,
And ring upon earth all evil's knell;
But now I wot if ye scour not well,
Red rust shall grow on God's great bell,
  And grass in the streets of God."

Ceased Alfred; and above his head
  The grand green domes, the Downs,

Showed the first legions of the press,
Marching in haste and bitterness
   For Christ's sake and the crown's.

Beyond the cavern of Colan,
   Past Eldred's by the sea,
Rose men that owned King Alfred's rod,
From the windy wastes of Exe untrod,
Or where the thorn of the grave of God,
   Burns over Glastonbury.

Far northward and far westward,
   The distant tribes drew nigh,
Plains beyond plains, fell behind fell,
That a man at sunset sees so well,
And the tiny coloured towns that dwell
   In the corners of the sky.

But dark and thick as thronged the host,
   With drum and torch and blade,
The still-eyed King sat pondering,
As one that watches a live thing,
   The scoured chalk; and he said:

"Though I give this land to Our Lady,
   That helped me in Athelney,
Though lordlier trees and lustier sod
And happier hills hath no flesh trod

Than the garden of the Mother of God
  Between Thames side and the sea,

" I know that weeds shall grow in it
  Faster than men can burn;
And though they scatter now and go,
In some far century, sad and slow,
I have a vision, and I know
  The heathen shall return.

"They shall not come with war-ships,
  They shall not waste with brands,
But books be all their eating,
  And ink be on their hands.

"Not with the humour of hunters,
  Or savage skill in war,
But ordering all things with dead words,
Strings shall they make of beasts and birds,
  And wheels of wind and star.

"They shall come mild as a monkish clerk,
  With many a scroll and pen;
And backward shall ye wonder and gaze,
Desiring one of Alfred's days,
  When pagans still were men.

"The dear sun dwarfed of dreadful suns,
  Like fiercer flowers on stalk,

127

Earth lost and little like a pea,
In high heaven's towering forestry
— These be the small weeds ye shall see
    Crawl, covering the chalk.

"But though they bridge St. Mary's sea
    Or steal St. Michael's wing —
Though they rear marvels over us,
Greater than great Vergilius
    Wrought for the Roman king;

"By this sign you shall know them,
    The breaking of the sword,
And Man no more a free knight,
    That loves or hates his lord.

"Yea, this shall be the sign of them,
    The sign of the dying fire,
And Man made like a half-wit,
    That knows not of his sire.

"What though they come with scroll and pen,
    And grave as a shaven clerk,
By this sign you shall know them,
    That they ruin and make dark;

"By all men bound to Nothing,
    Being slaves without a lord,

THE SCOURING OF THE HORSE

By one blind idiot world obeyed,
   Too blind to be abhorred;

"By terror and the cruel tales
   Of curse in bone and kin,
By weird and weakness winning,
Accursed from the beginning,
By detail of the sinning
   And denial of the sin;

"By thought a crawling ruin,
   By life a leaping mire,
By a broken heart in the breast of the world,
   And the end of the world's desire;

"By God and man dishonoured,
   By death and life made vain,
Know ye the old barbarian,
   The barbarian come again —

"When is great talk of trend and tide,
   And wisdom and destiny,
Hail that undying heathen
   That is sadder than the sea.

"In what wise men shall smite him,
   Or the Cross stand up again,
Or charity or chivalry,

THE BALLAD OF THE WHITE HORSE

My vision saith not; and I see
No more; but now ride doubtfully
  To the battle of the plain."

And the grass-edge of the great down
  Was cut clean as a lawn,
While the levies thronged from near and far,
From the warm woods of the western star,
And the King went out to his last war
  On a tall grey horse at dawn.

And news of his far-off fighting
  Came slow and brokenly,
From the land of the East Saxons,
  From the sunrise and the sea.

From the plains of the white sunrise,
  And sad St. Edmund's crown,
Where the pools of Essex pale and gleam
  Out beyond London town —

In mighty and doubtful fragments,
  Like faint or fabled wars,
Climbed the old hills of his renown,
Where the bald brow of White Horse Down
  Is close to the cold stars.

But away in the eastern places
  The wind of death walked high,

THE SCOURING OF THE HORSE

And a raid was driven athwart the raid,
The sky reddened and the smoke swayed,
  And the tall grey horse went by.

The gates of the great river
  Were breached as with a barge,
The walls sank crowded, say the scribes,
And high towers populous with tribes
  Seemed leaning from the charge.

Smoke like rebellious heavens rolled
  Curled over coloured flames,
Mirrored in monstrous purple dreams,
  In the mighty pools of Thames.

Loud was the war on London wall,
  And loud in London gates,
And loud the sea-kings in the cloud,
Broke through their dreaming gods, and loud
  Cried on their dreadful Fates.

And all the while on White Horse Hill,
  The horse lay long and wan,
The turf crawled and the fungus crept,
And the little sorrel, while all men slept,
  Unwrought the work of man.

With velvet finger, velvet foot,
  The fierce soft mosses then

THE BALLAD OF THE WHITE HORSE

Crept on the large white commonweal
All folk had striven to strip and peel,
And the grass, like a great green witch's wheel,
  Unwound the toils of men.

And clover and silent thistle throve,
  And buds burst silently,
With little care for the Thames Valley,
  Or what things there might be —

That away on the widening river,
  In the eastern plains for crown
Stood up in the pale purple sky
One turret of smoke like ivory;
And the smoke changed and the wind went by,
  And the King took London Town.